Johann Sebastian Bach for Man

MW00447059

Contents

Bourrée Angloise 4

Marche *(Allegro)* 7

Fantaisie 8

Marche *(Allegro ma non troppo)* 14

Courante 16

Passepied I (en Rondeau) 18

Air 22

Gavotte I 24

Gavotta 26

Gigue 28

Suite III 31

Allemande 37

Courante 40

Sarabande 44

Bouree I 46

Bouree II 48

Gigue 50

Ciaccona 56

Bouree 80

Menuet 82

Sarabande 84

Bourée I 86

Bourée II 88

Giga 89

Violin Concerto No. in A minor 92

Sarabanda 102

Bourrée Angloise

(from Partita in A minor for solo flute)

Johann Sebastian Bach
(1685 - 1750)

Vivace

m e l b a y p r e s e n t s

J. S. Bach for Mandolin

by Robert Bancalari

CD CONTENTS

Track		Page	Duration	Track		Page	Duration
1	Marche — in D Major	7	[:59]	8	Courante — in F Major	16	[2:03]
2	Marche — in G Major	14	[1:38]	9	Bouree — in D Major	80	[1:12]
3	Menuet — in D minor	82	[:52]	10	Gavotta — in E minor	26	[1:55]
4	Air — in E♭ Major	22	[2:53]	11	Fantaisie — in A minor	8	[1:56]
5	Sarabande — in B minor	84	[2:16]	12	Bourrée Angloise — in A minor	4	[2:37]
6	Bourée — in B minor (I and II)	86 & 88	[1:47]	13	Bouree — in G Major	46	[1:29]
7	Gavotte — in G minor	24	[1:31]				

13 Solos from the book have been recorded on the enclosed CD.

1 2 3 4 5 6 7 8 9 0

Visit us on the Web at www.melbay.com — E-mail us at email@melbay.com

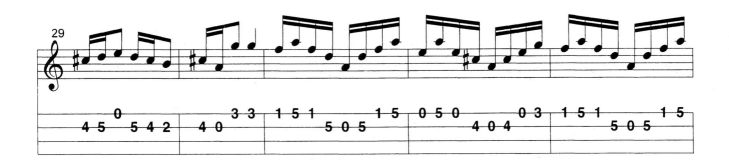

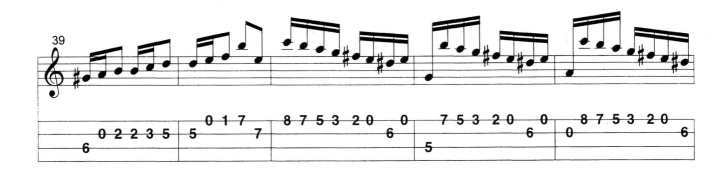

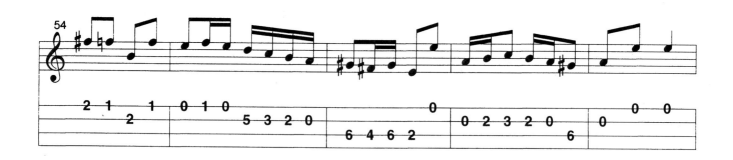

Marche

(from the Anna Magdalena Bach Book)

Johann Sebastian Bach
(1685 - 1750)

Allegro

Fantaisie

(from Partita No. III in A minor)

Johann Sebastian Bach
(1685 - 1750)

Allegro Moderato

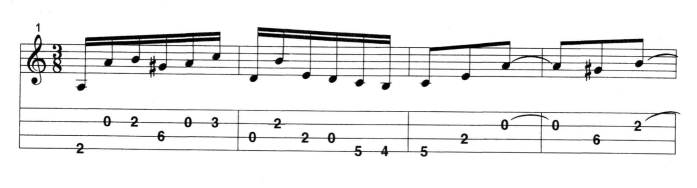

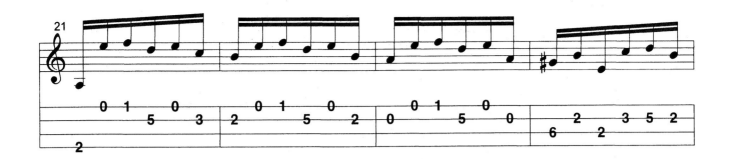

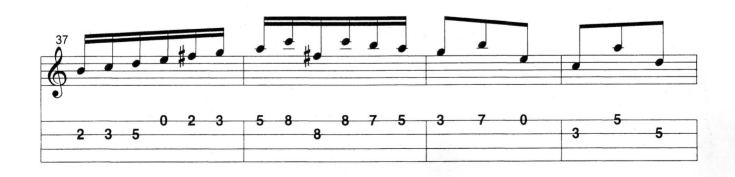

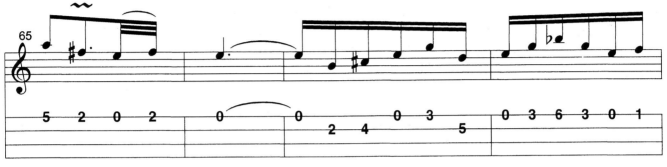

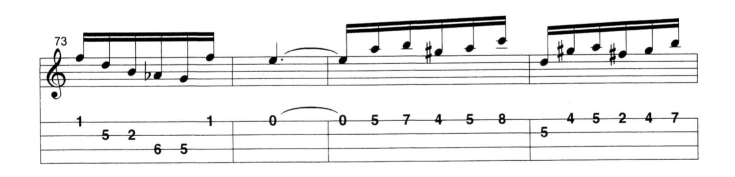

Marche

(from the Anna Magdalena Bach Book)

Johann Sebastian Bach
(1685 - 1750)

Allegro ma non troppo

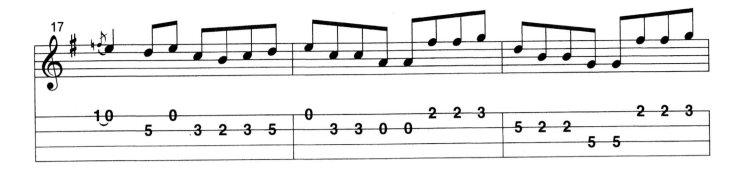

Courante

(from English Suite No. IV in F)

Johann Sebastian Bach
(1685 - 1750)

Allegro

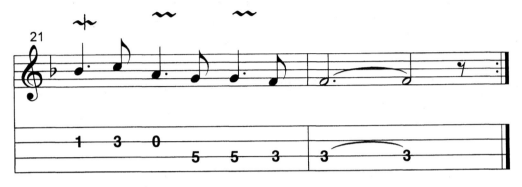

Passepied I (en Rondeau)
(from English Suite No. V in E minor)

Johann Sebastian Bach
(1685 - 1750)

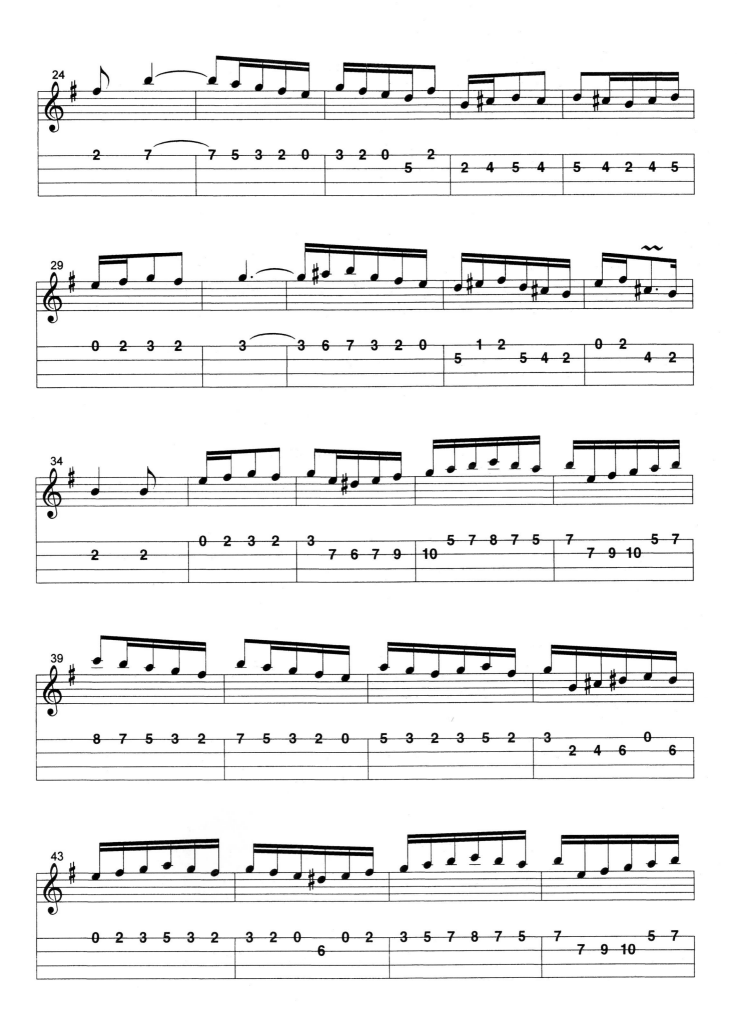

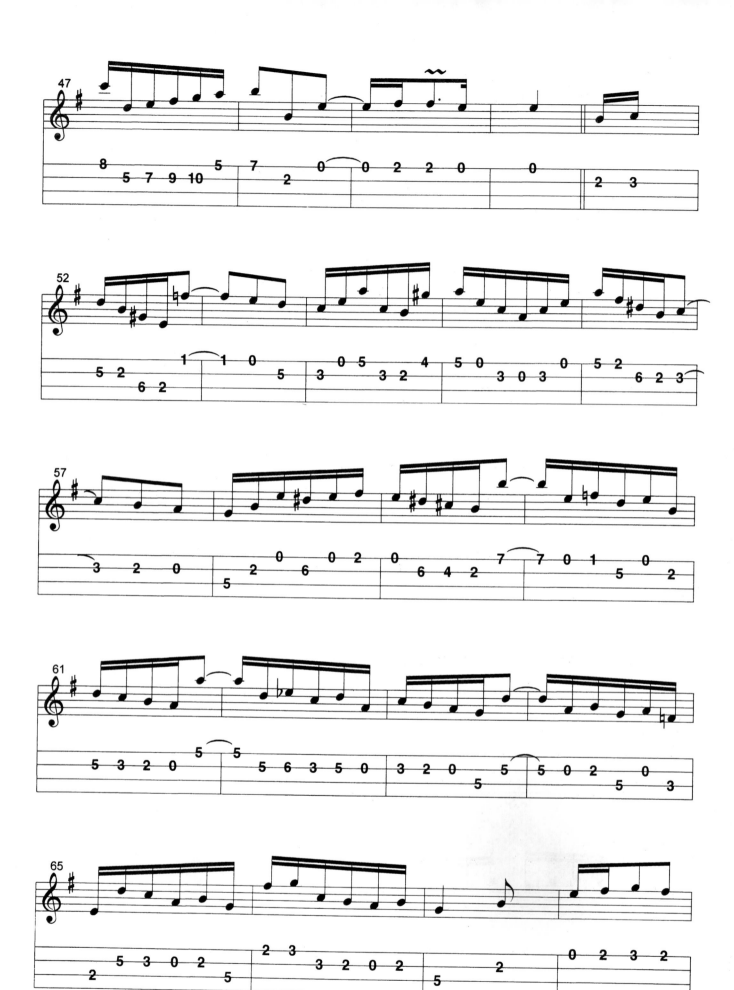

Air

(from French Suite No. IV in Eb)

Johann Sebastian Bach
(1685 - 1750)

Moderato

Gavotte I
(from English Suite No. III in G Minor)

Johann Sebastian Bach
(1685 - 1750)

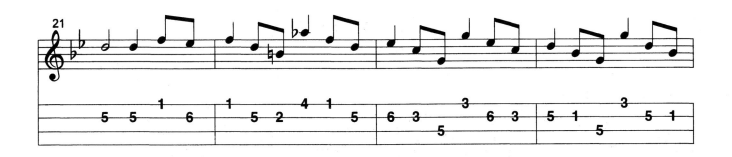

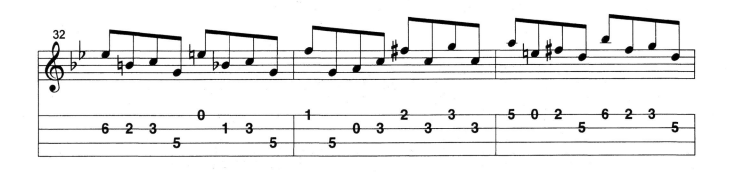

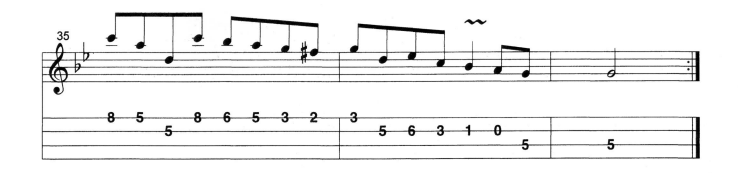

Gavotta

(from Partita No. VI in E minor)

Johann Sebastian Bach
(1685 - 1750)

Un Poco Allegro

27

Gigue

(from French Suite No. VI in E)

Johann Sebastian Bach
(1685 - 1750)

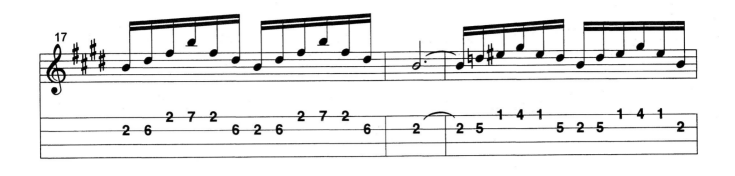

Suite III

(from solo Suites for Cello)

Prelude

Johann Sebastian Bach
(1685 - 1750)

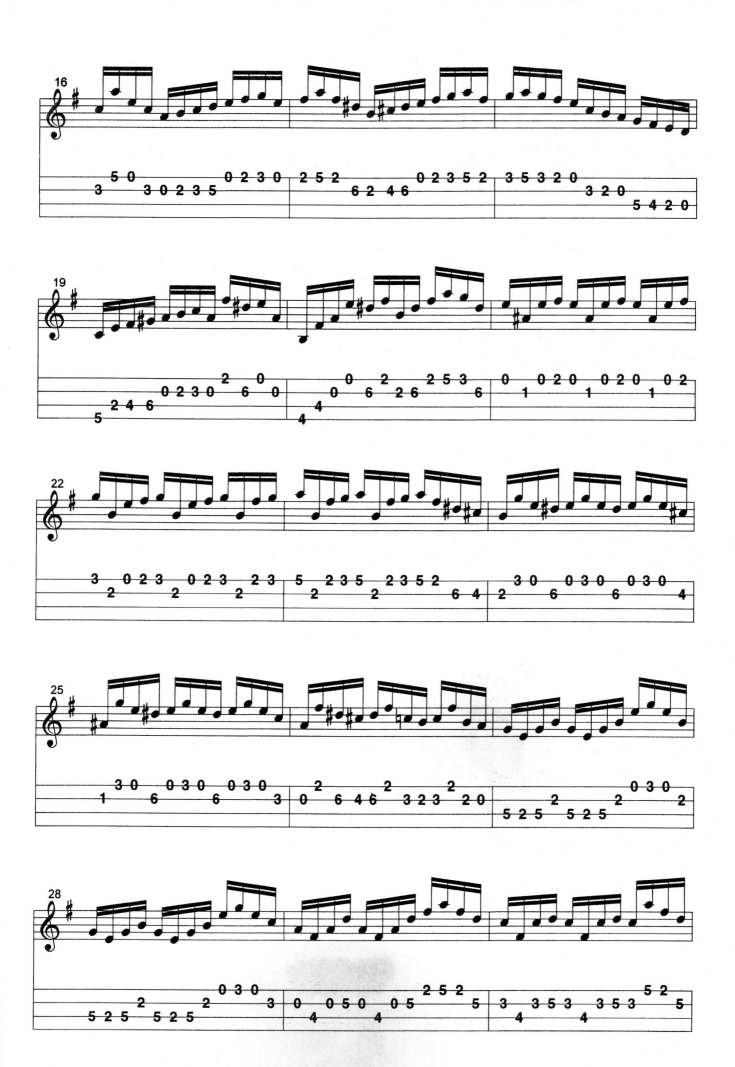

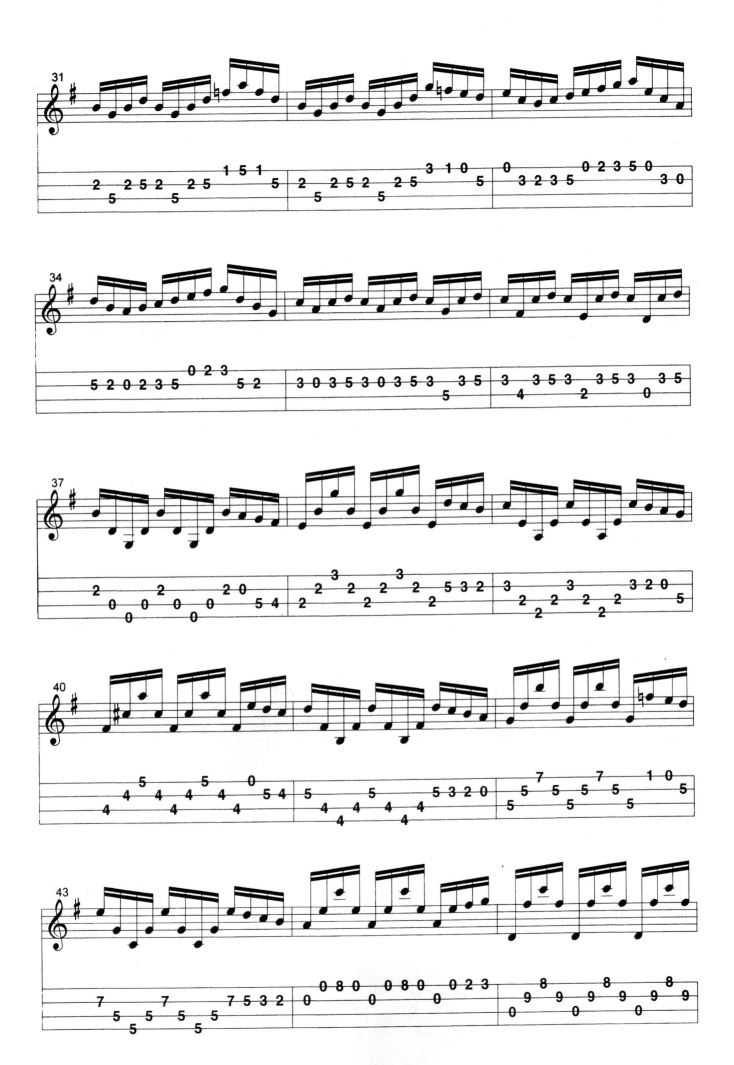

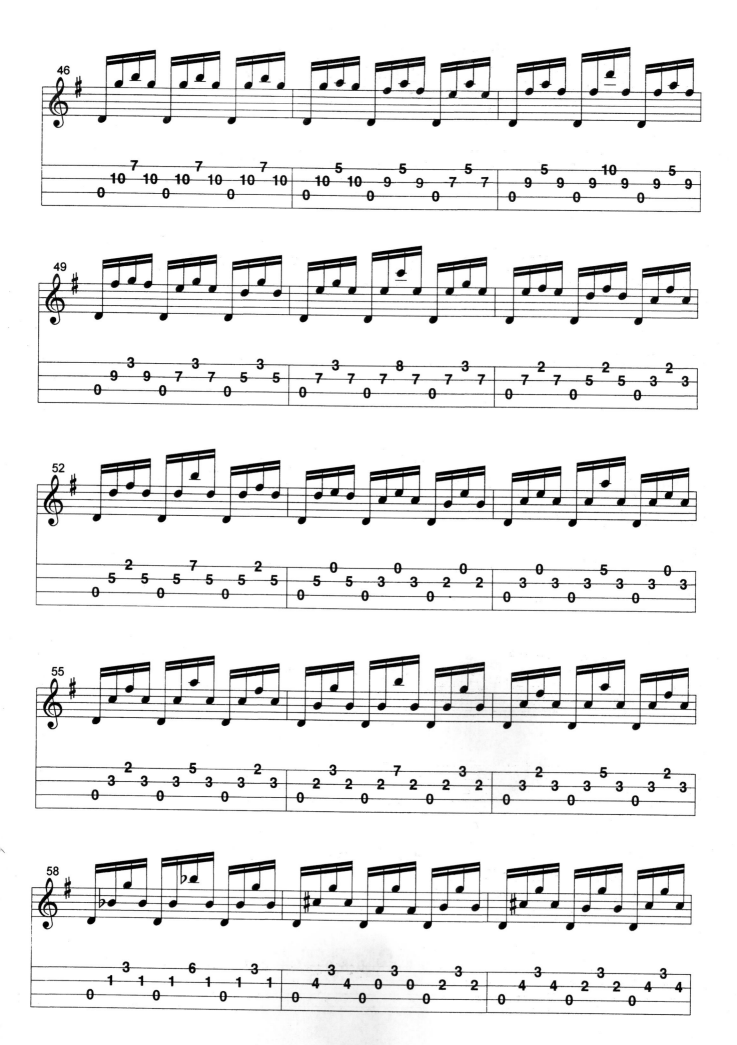

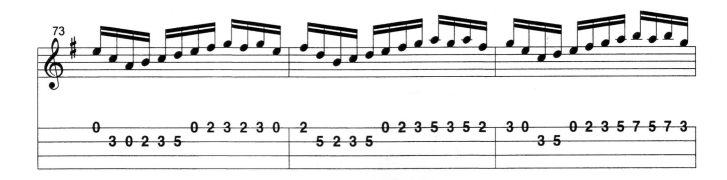

Allemande

Johann Sebastian Bach
(1685 - 1750)

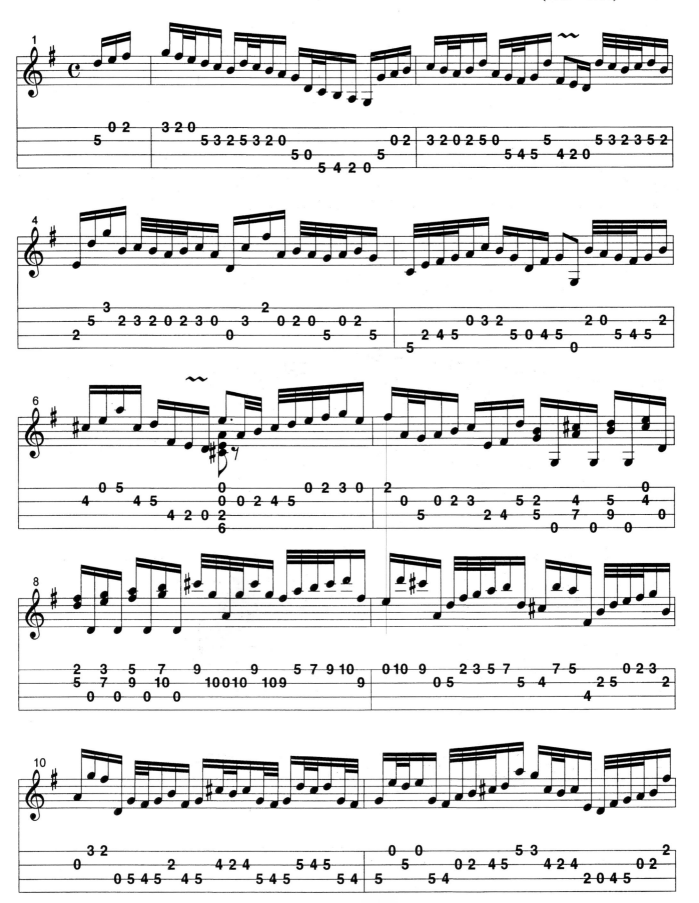

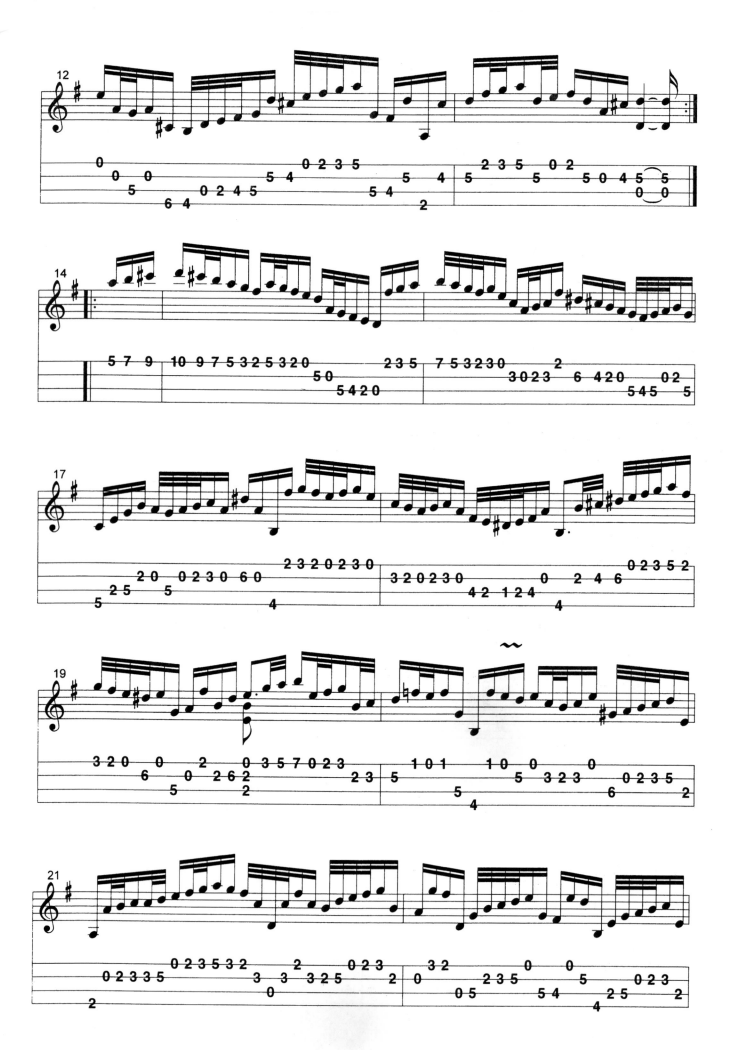

38

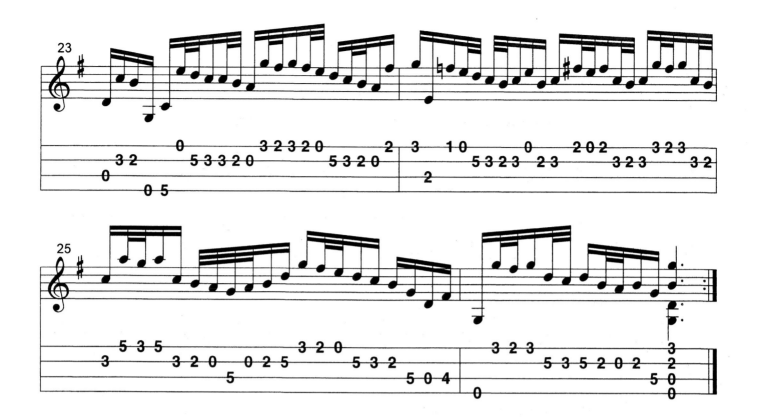

Courante

Johann Sebastian Bach
(1685 - 1750)

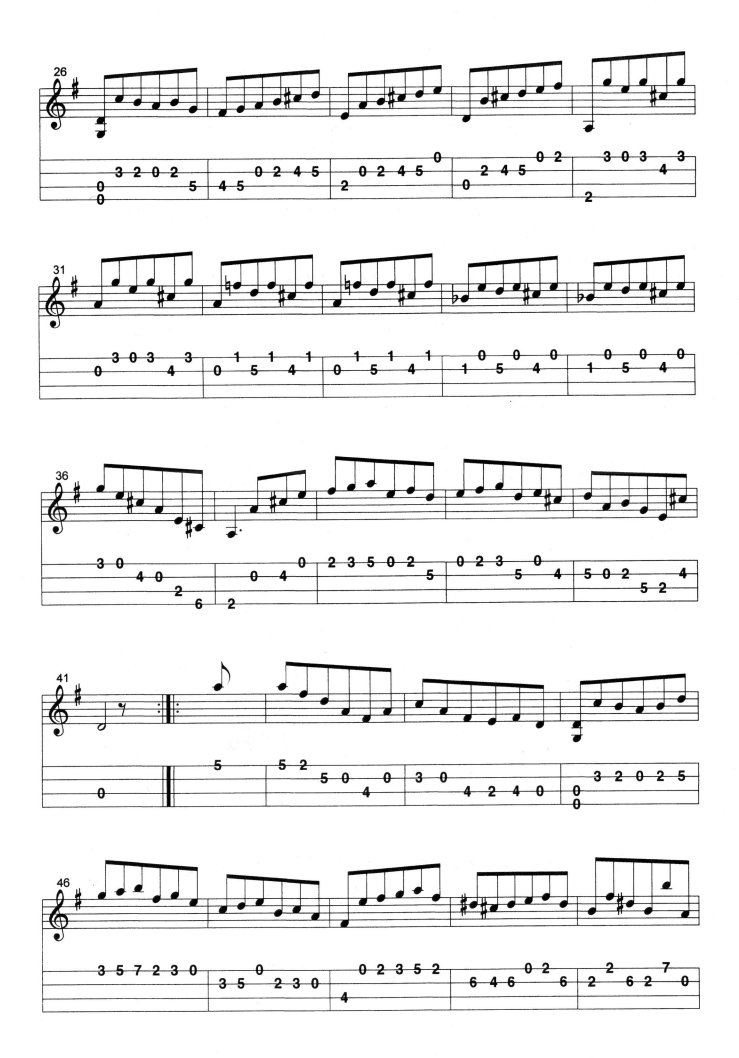

41

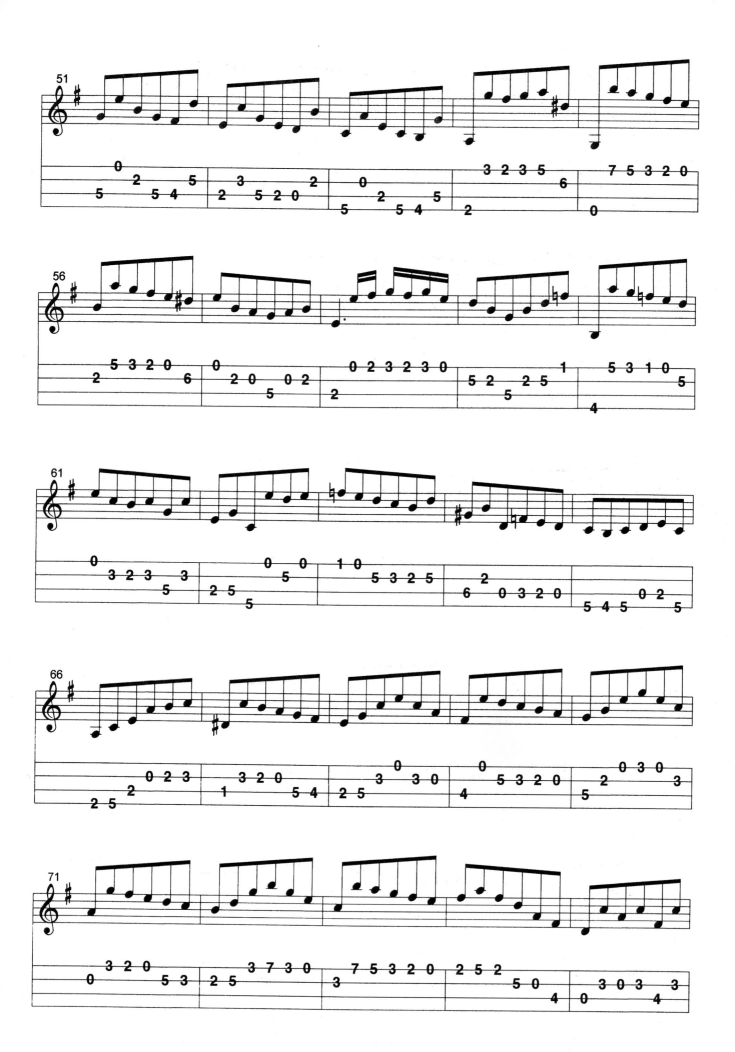

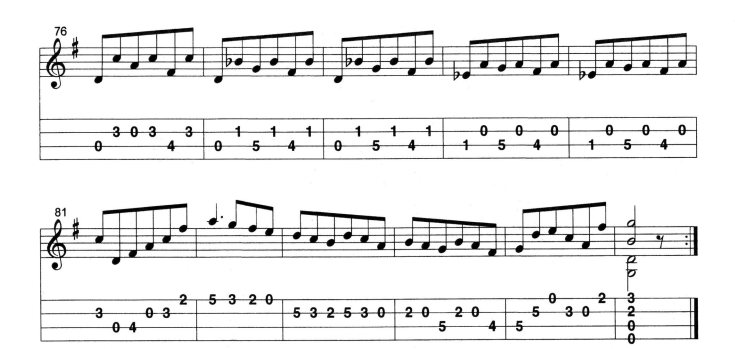

Sarabande

Johann Sebastian Bach
(1685 - 1750)

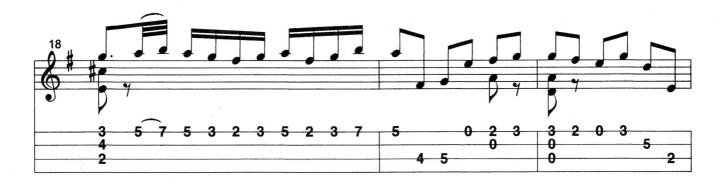

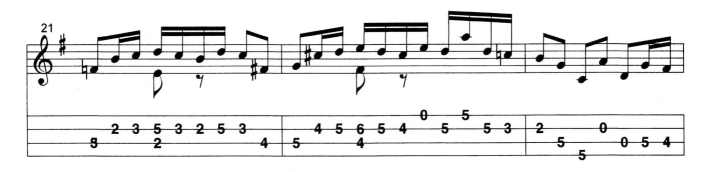

Bouree I

Johann Sebastian Bach
(1685 - 1750)

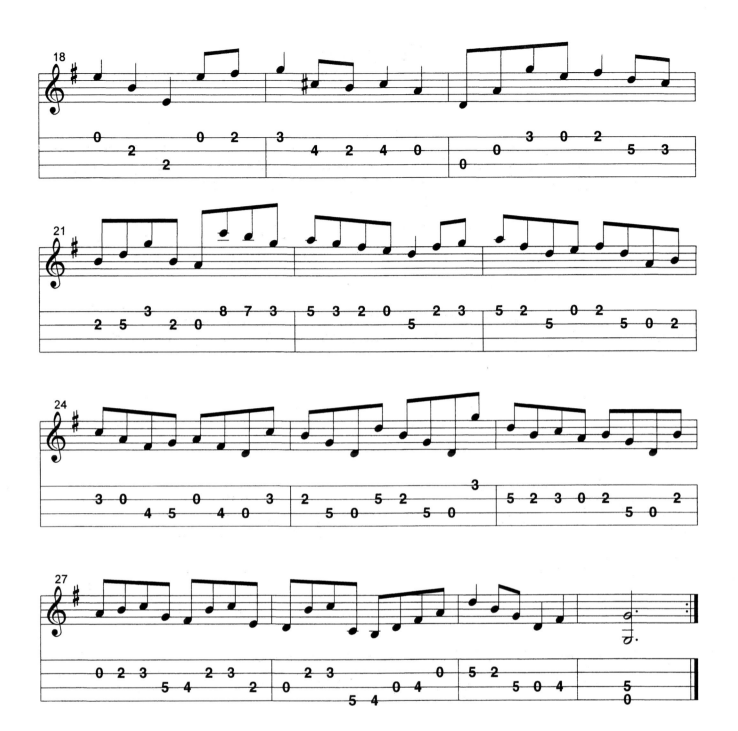

Bouree II

Johann Sebastian Bach
(1685 - 1750)

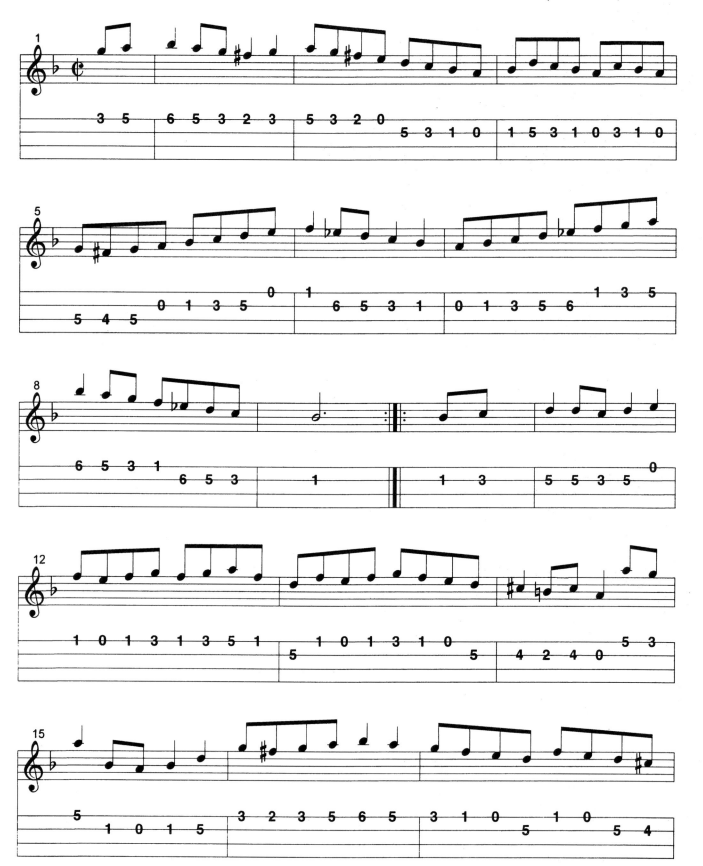

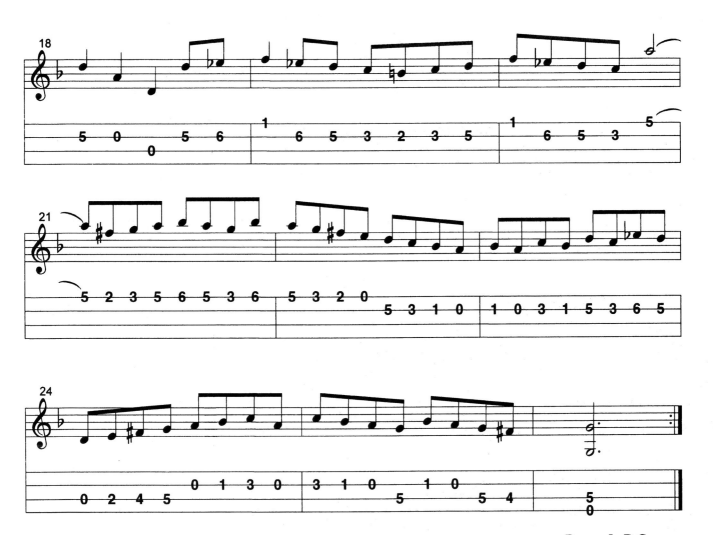

Bouree I   D.C.

Gigue

Johann Sebastian Bach
(1685 - 1750)

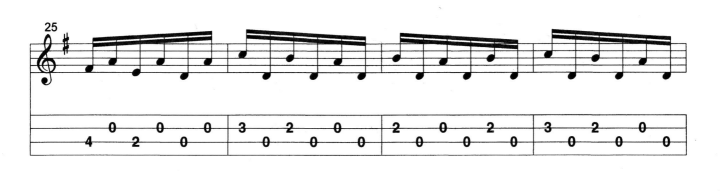

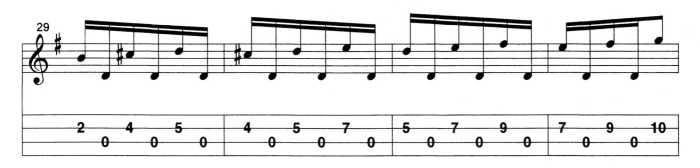

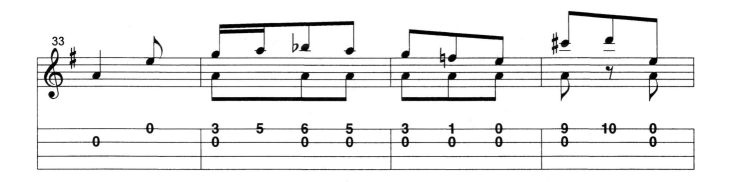

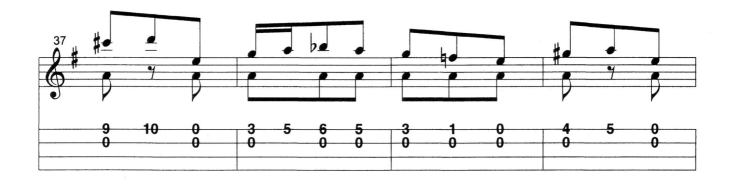

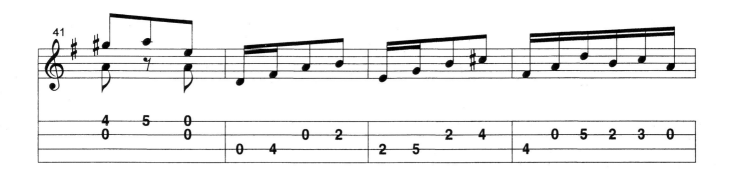

53

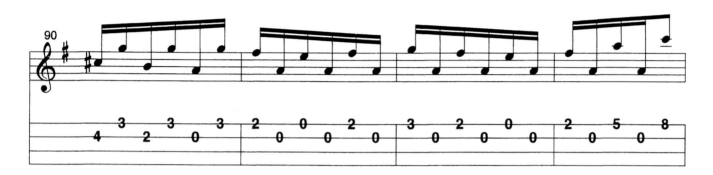

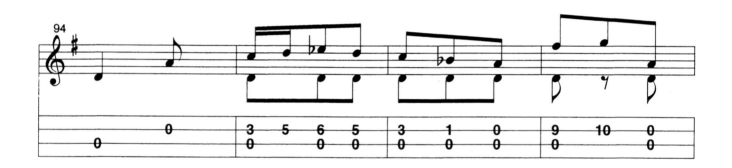

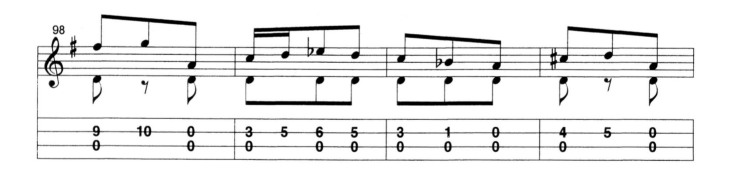

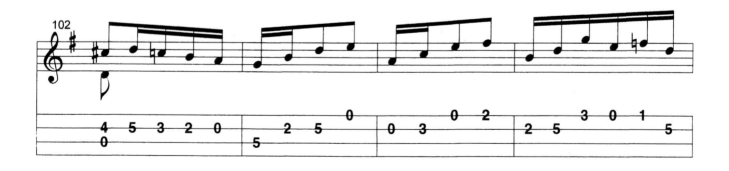

Ciaccona

(from Sonata No. 4 in D minor for solo violin)

Johann Sebastian Bach
(1685 - 1750)

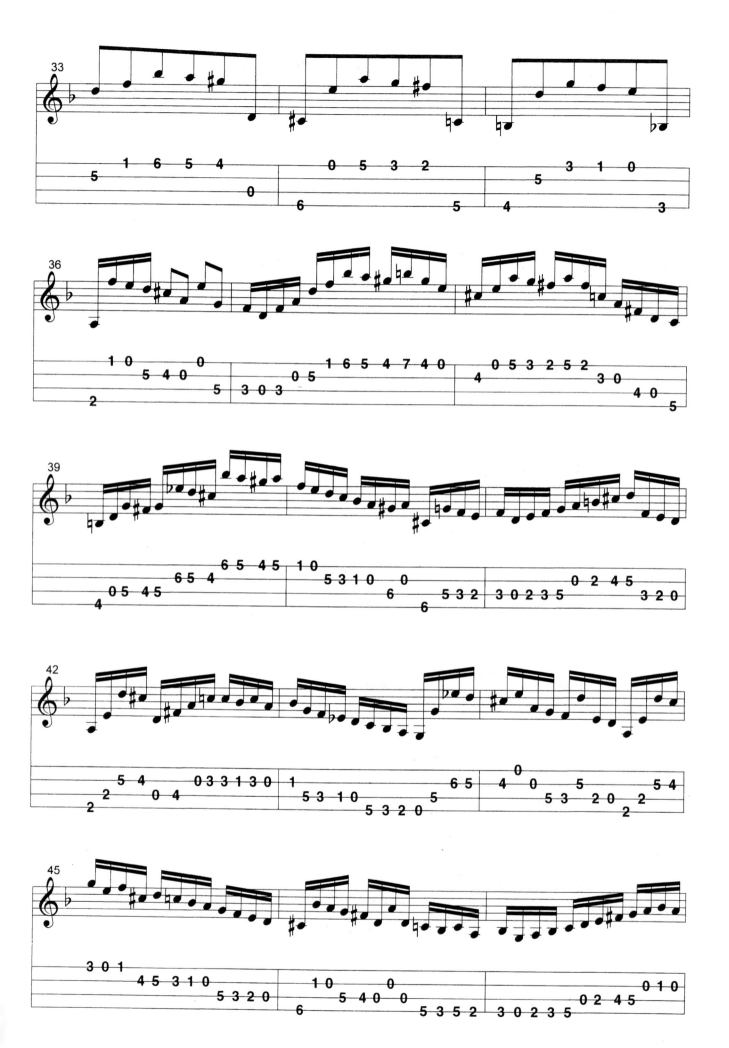

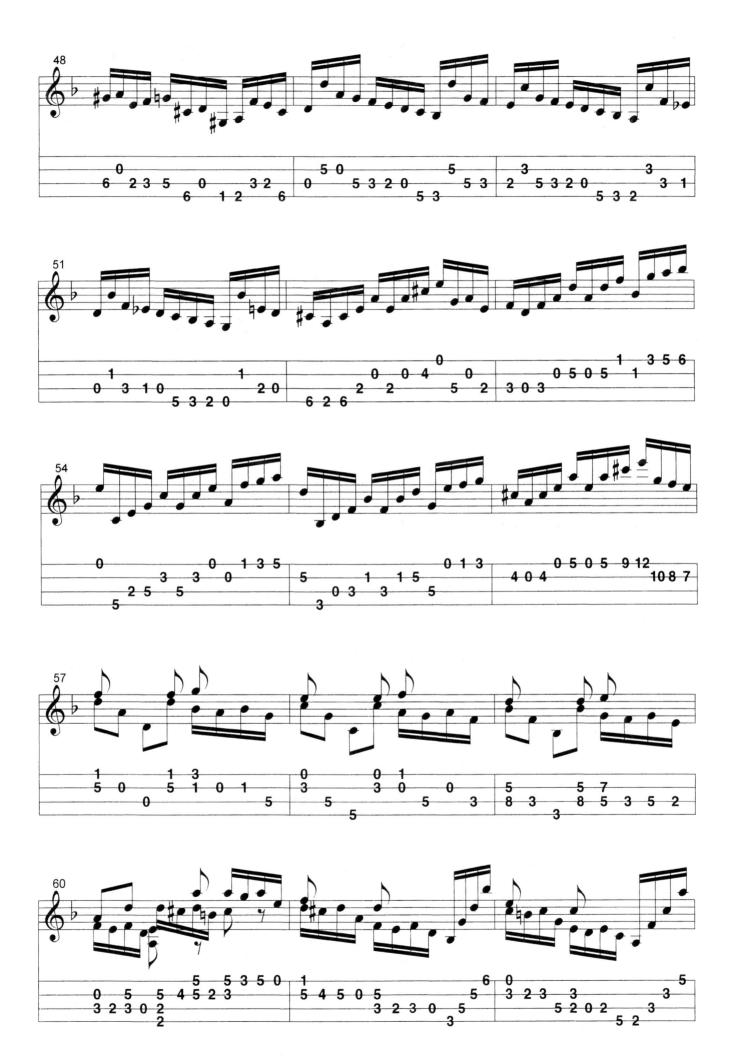

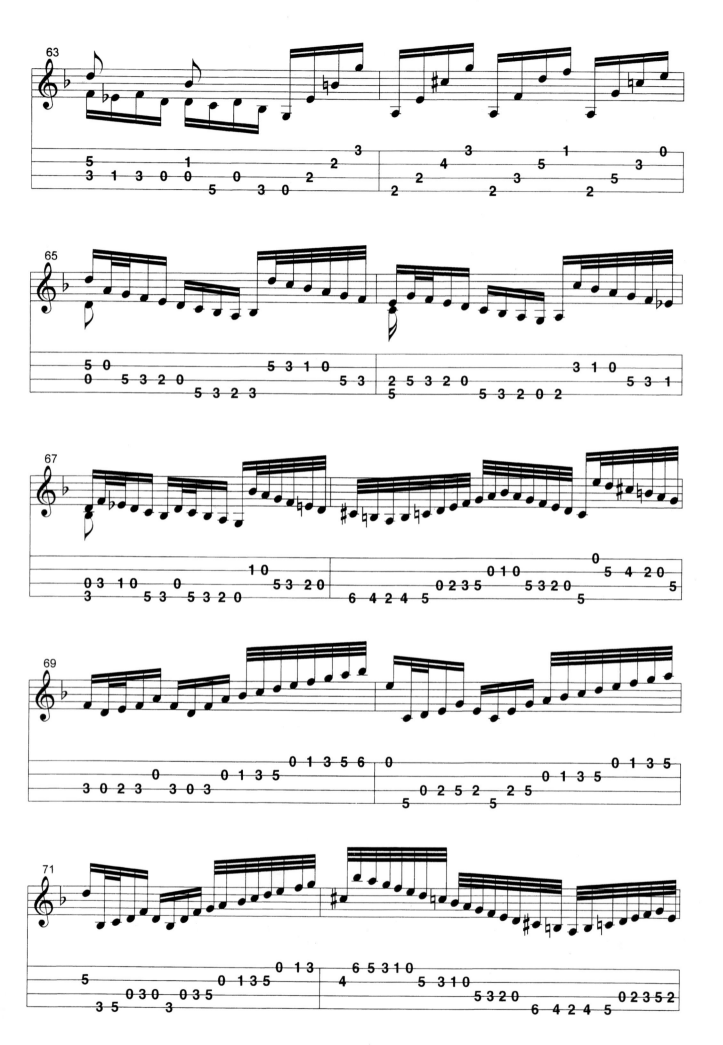

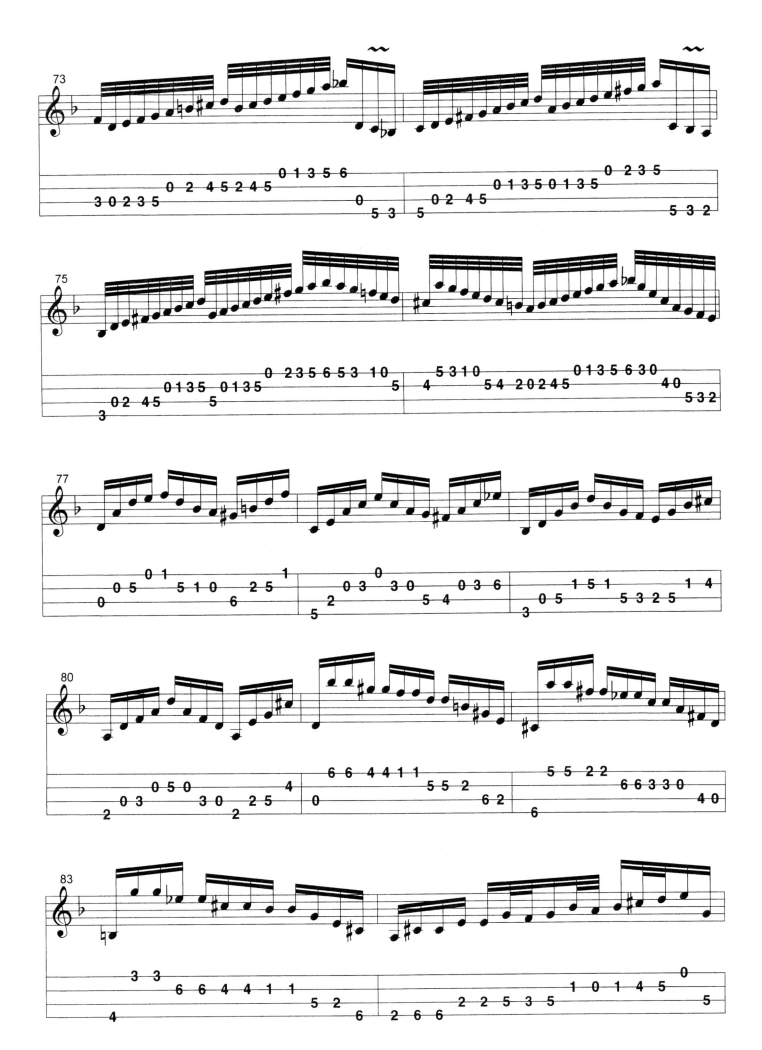

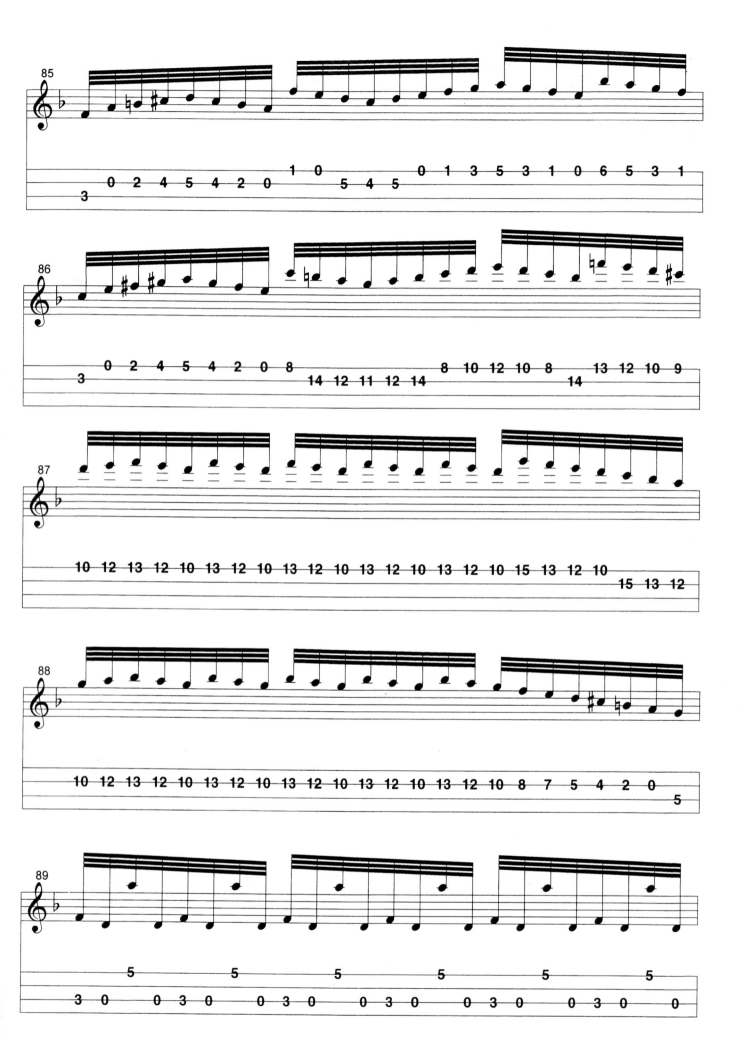

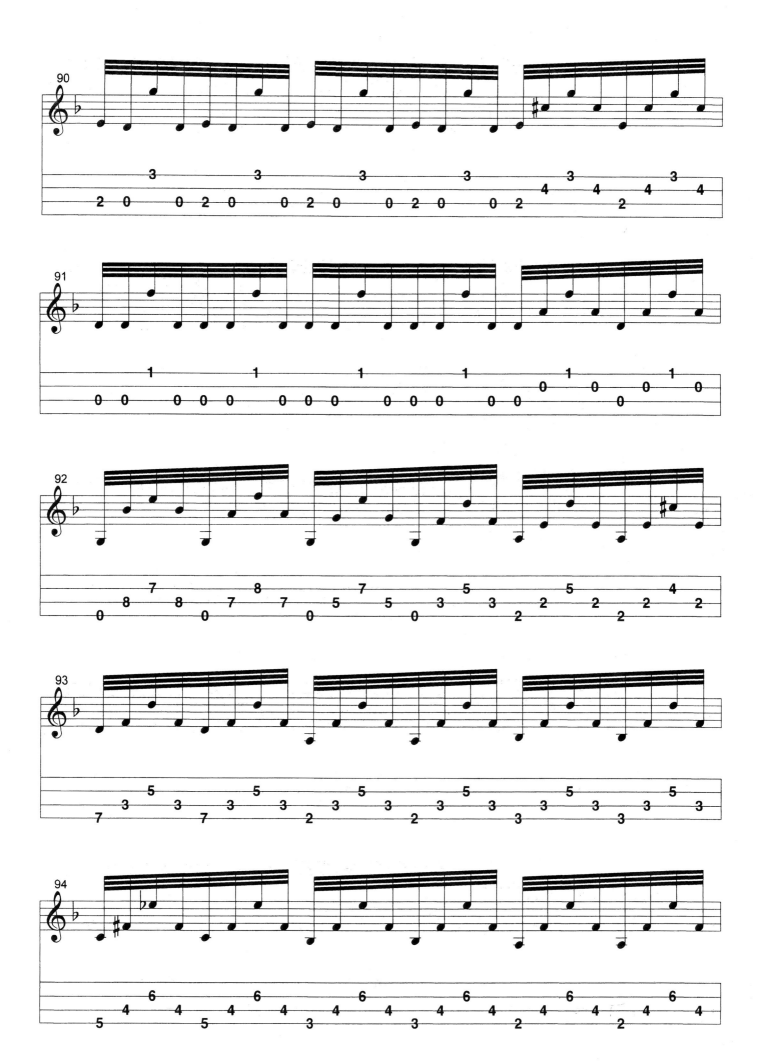

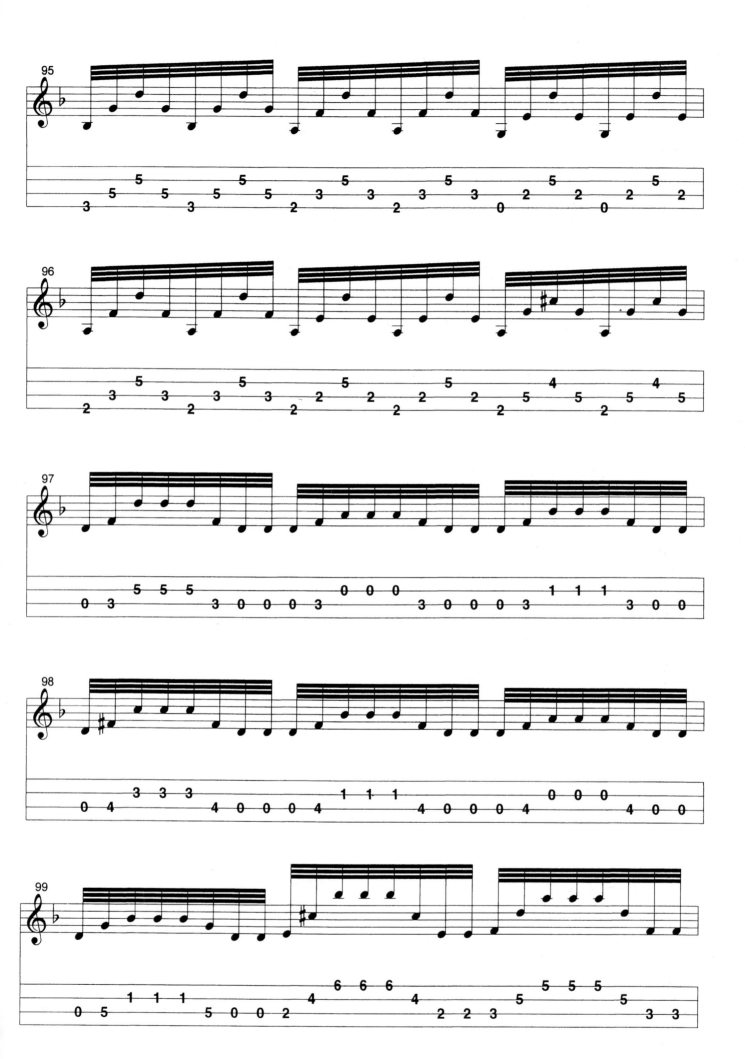

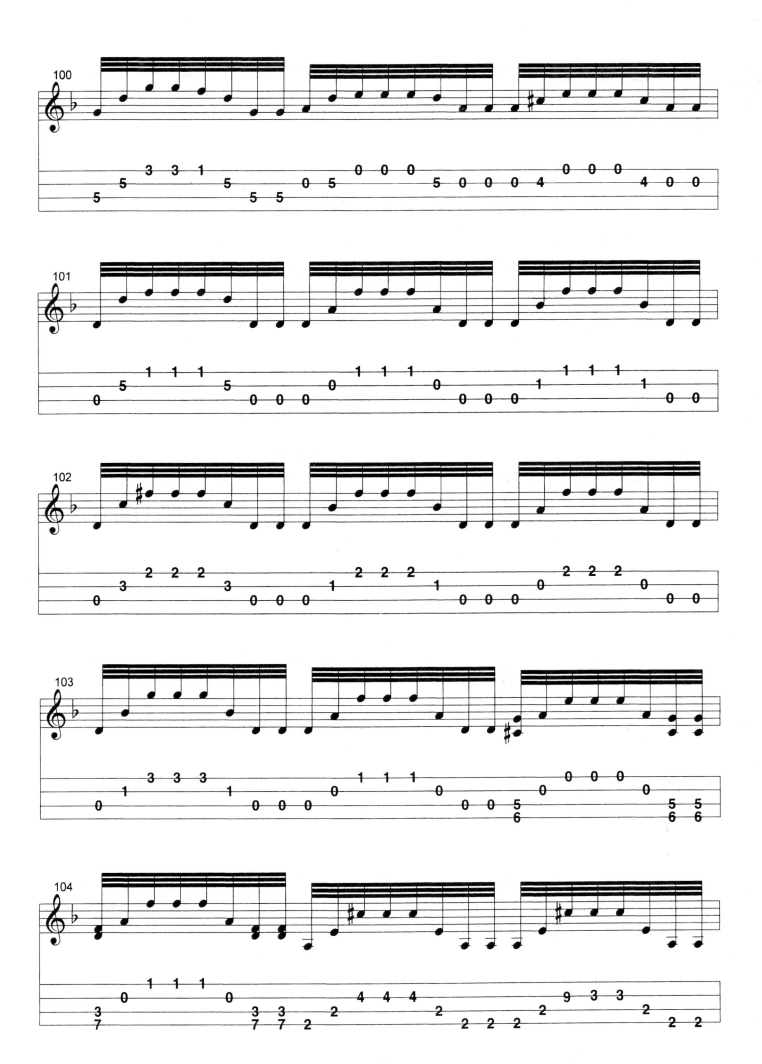

65

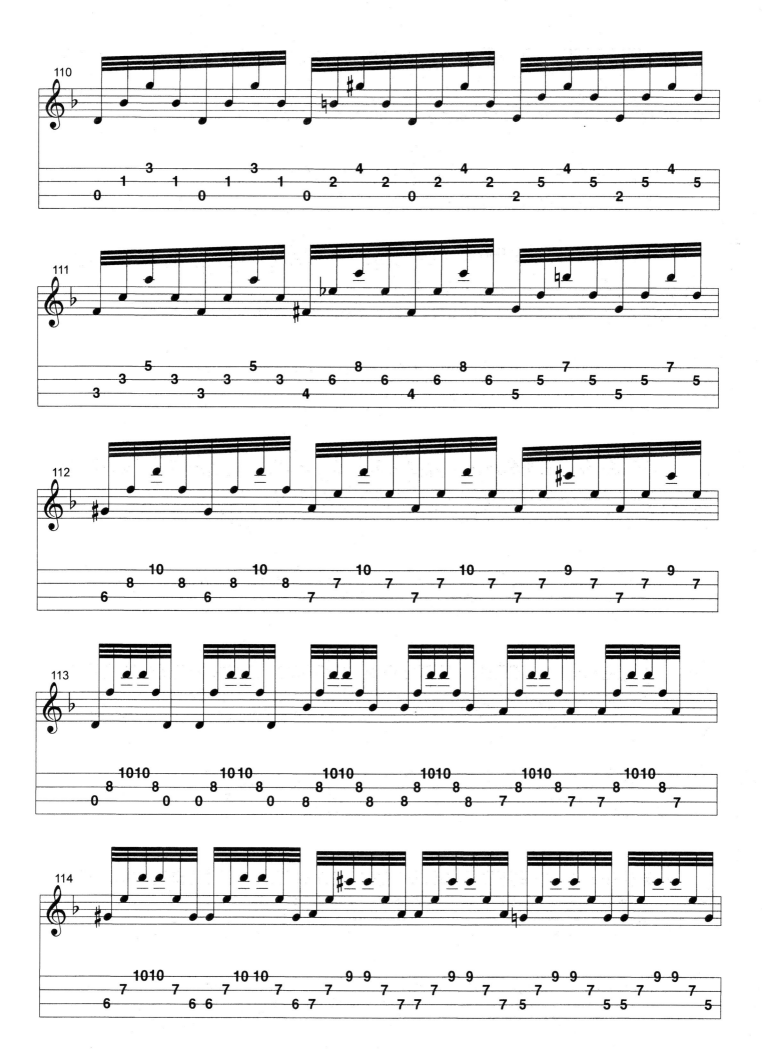

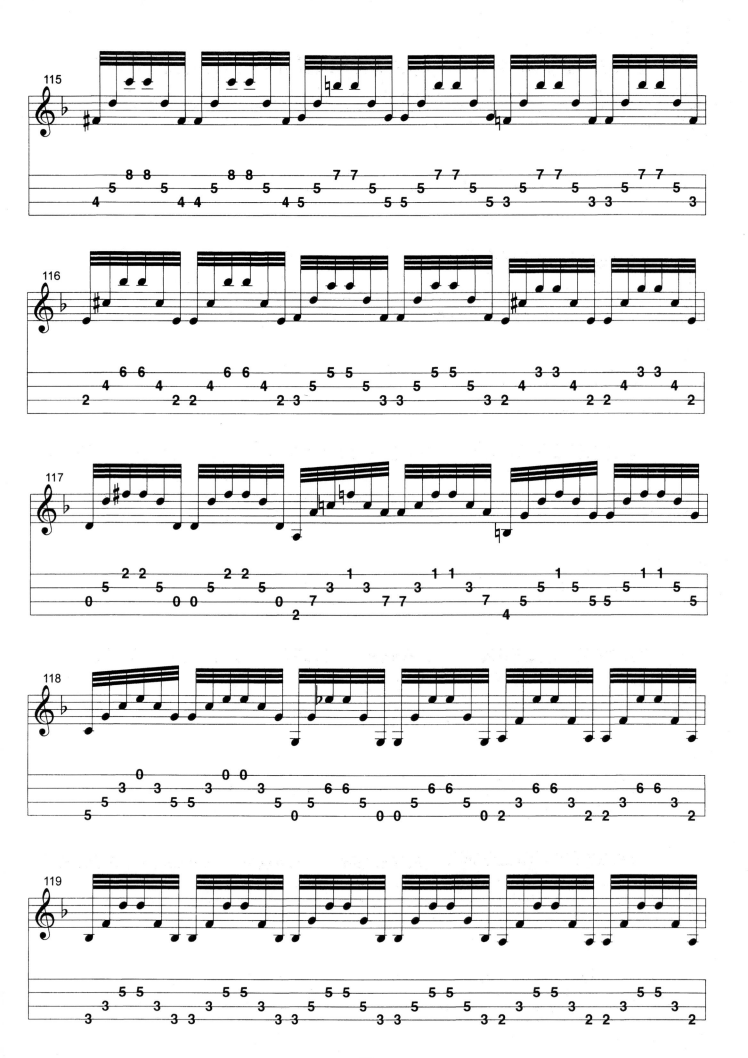

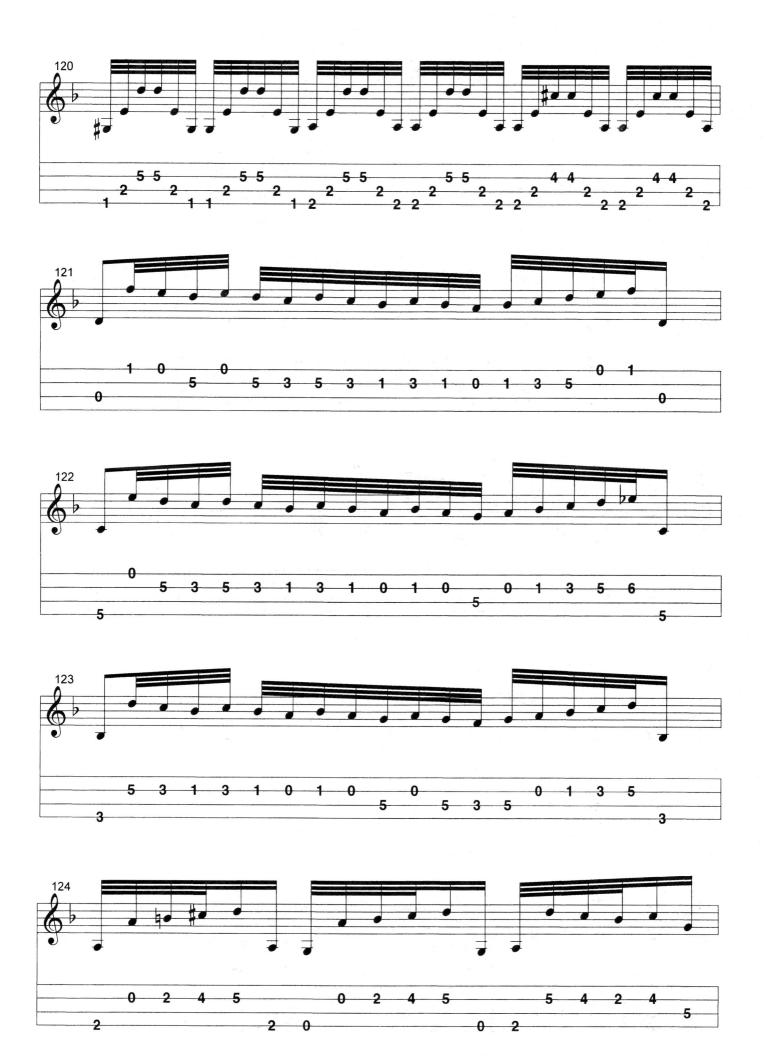

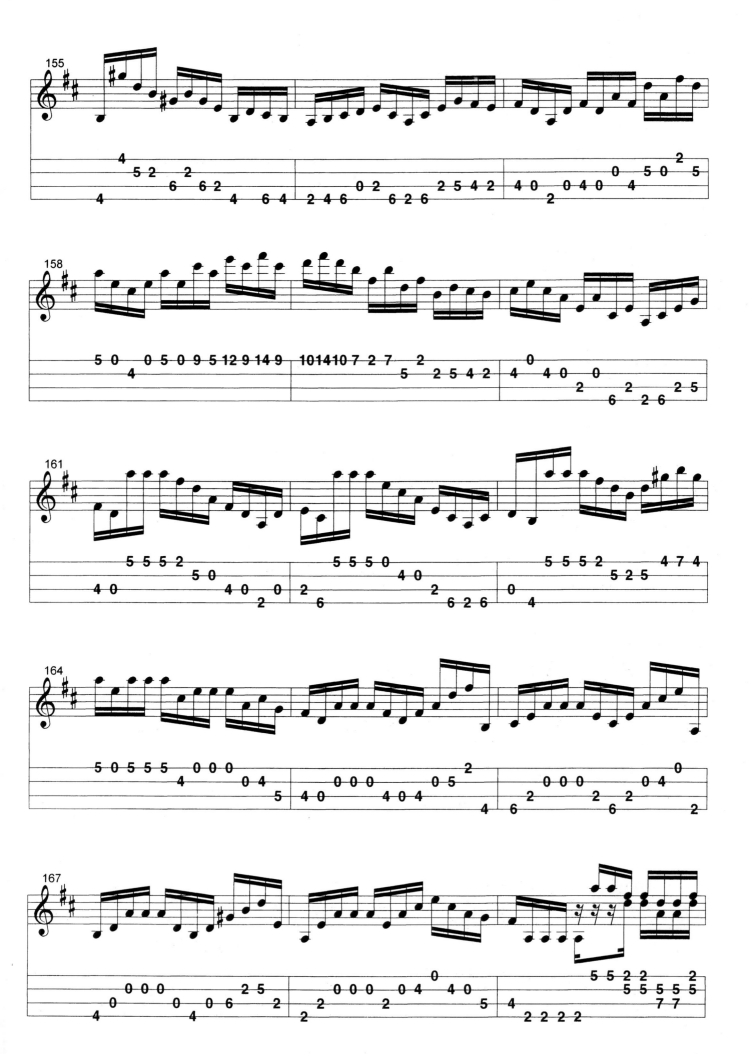

75

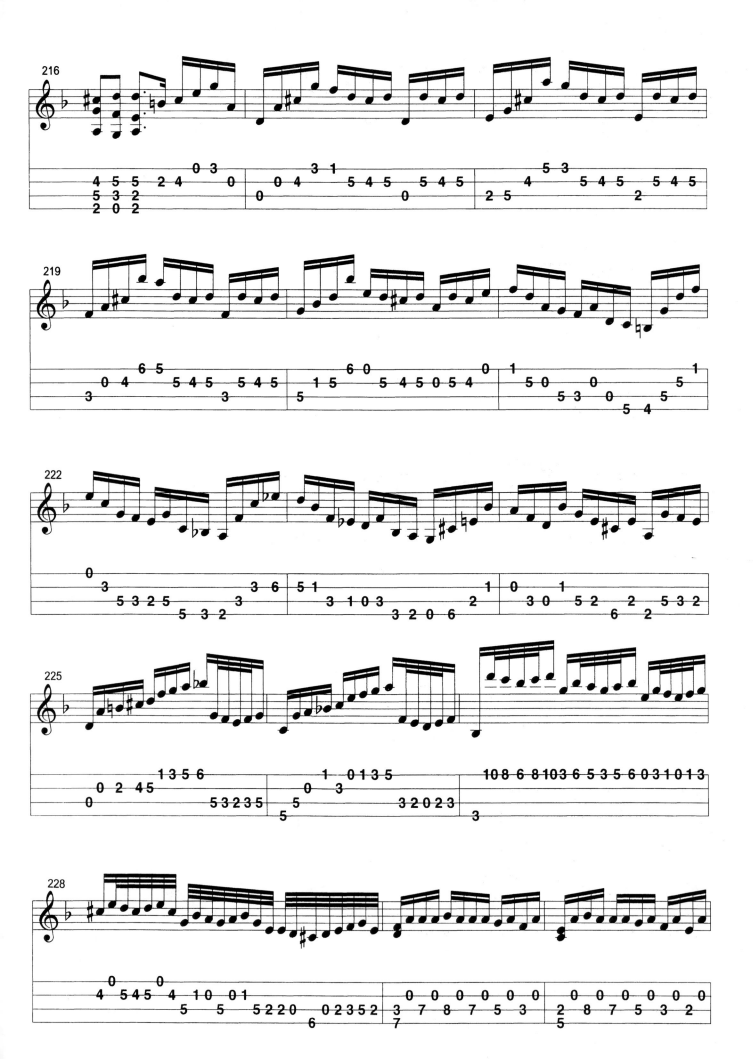

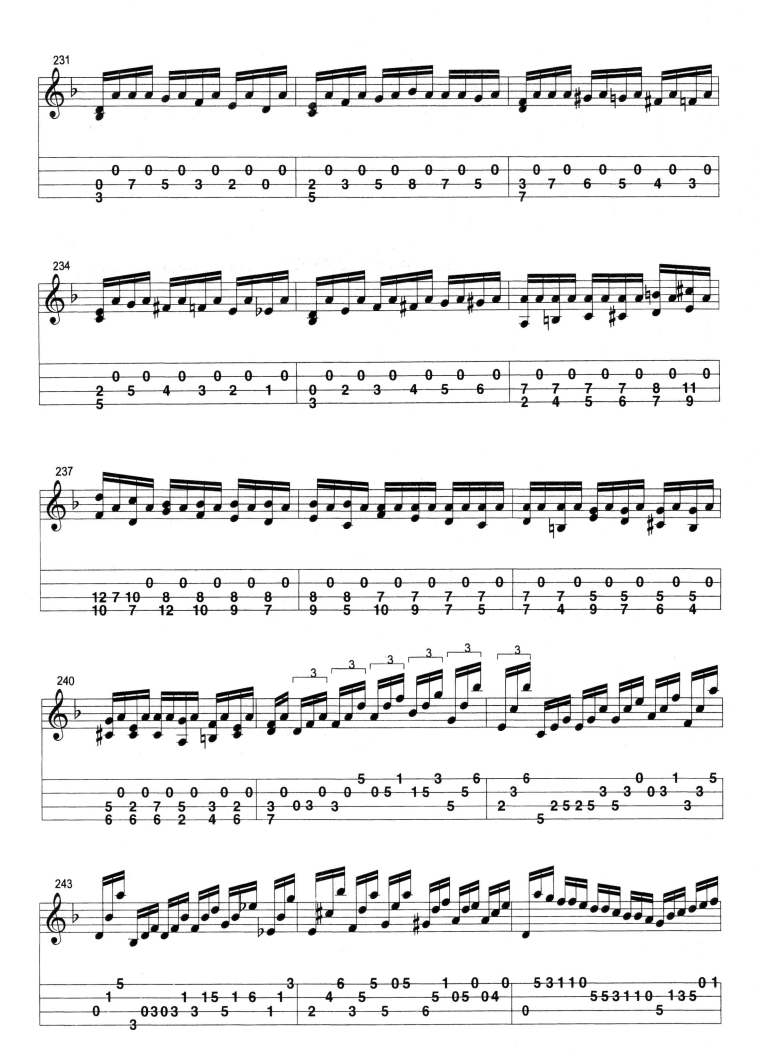

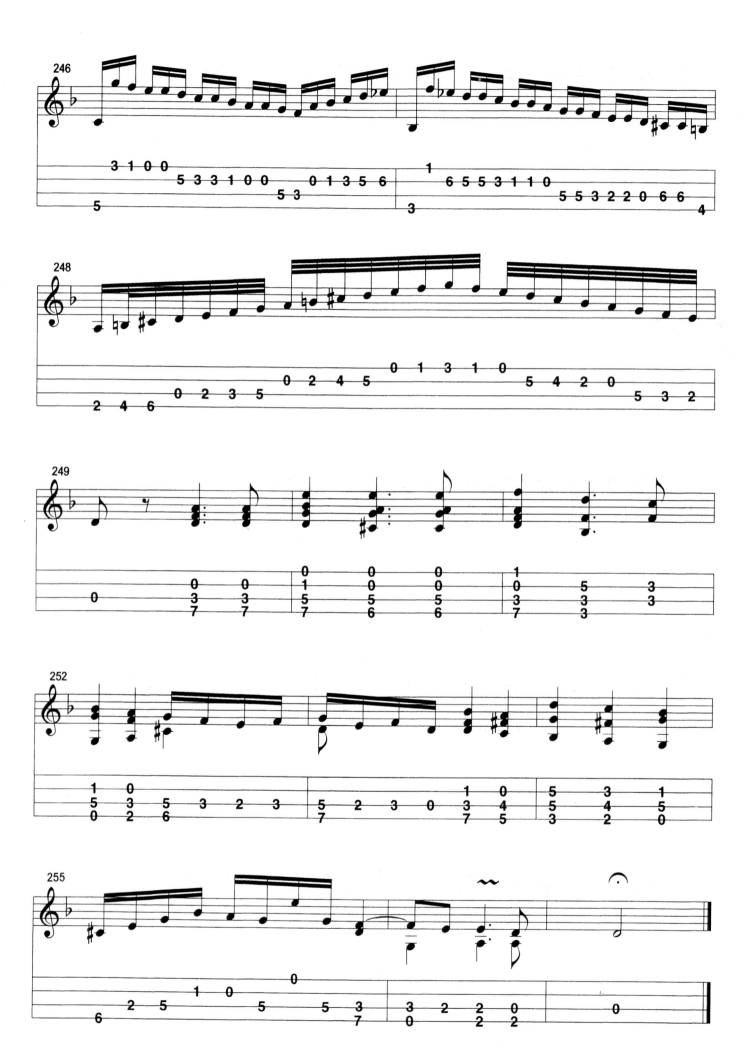

*This page has been
left blank to avoid
awkward page turns*

Bourrée

(from Orchestral Suite No. 3 in D)

Johann Sebastian Bach
(1685 - 1750)

Allegro

Menuet
(from Anna Magdalena Bach Book)

Johann Sebastian Bach
(1685 - 1750)

Sarabande

(from Orchestral Suite No. 2 in B minor)

Johann Sebastian Bach
(1685 - 1750)

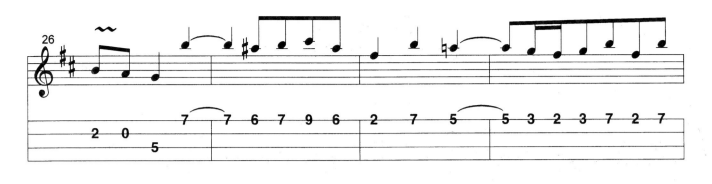

Bourrée I

(from Orchestral Suite No. 2 in B minor)

Johann Sebastian Bach
(1685 - 1750)

Bourrée II

(from Orchestral Suite No. 2 in B minor)

Johann Sebastian Bach
(1685 - 1750)

Bourrée I da Capo

Giga

(from Sonata # VI in E for solo violin)

Johann Sebastian Bach
(1685 - 1750)

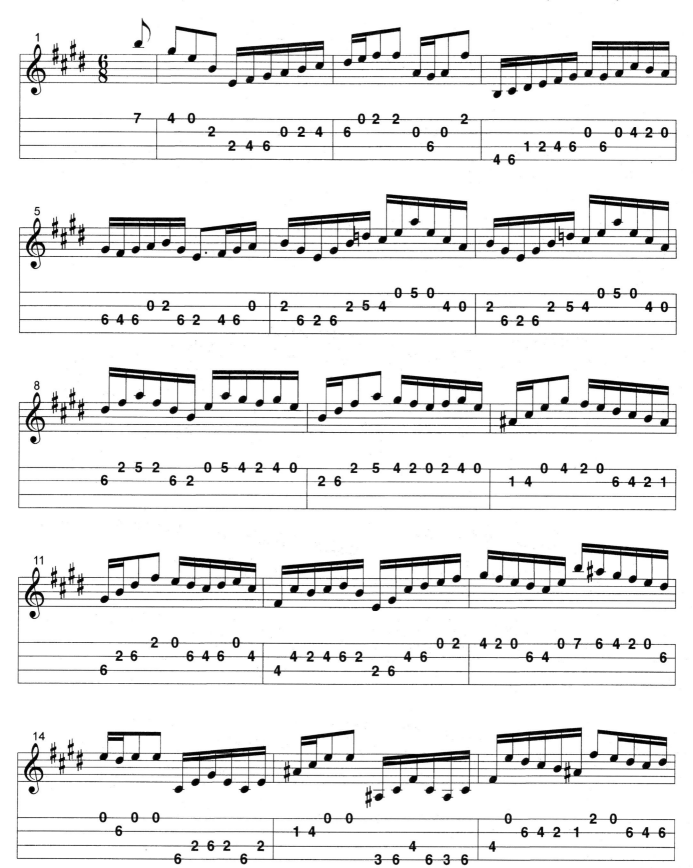

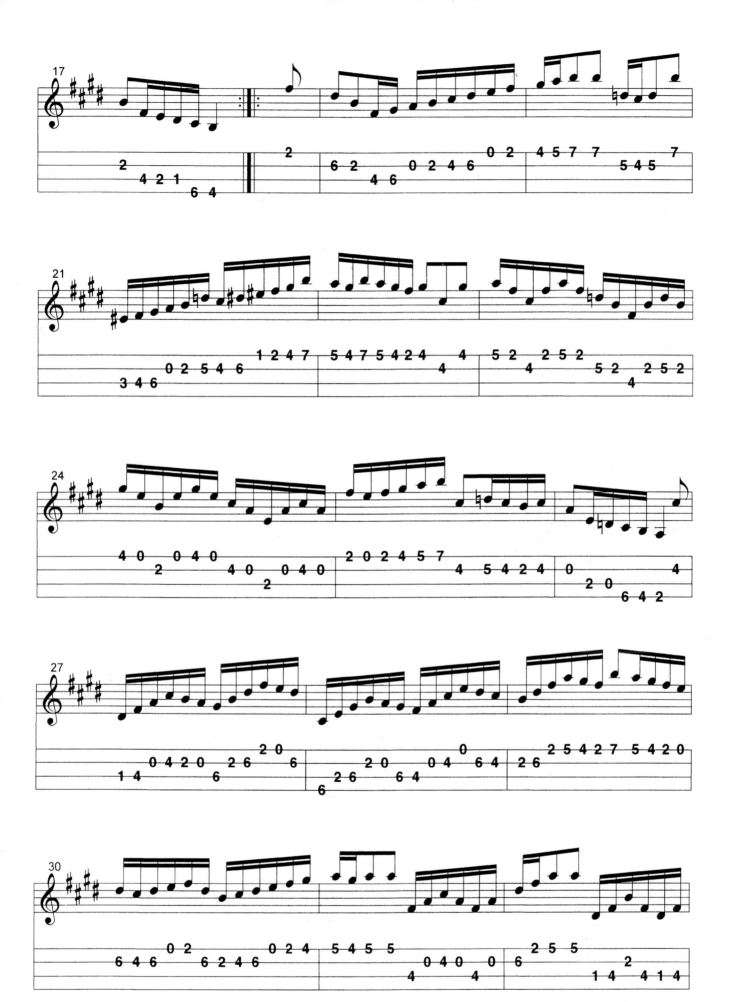

90

Violin Concerto No. I in A minor

(1st Movement)

Johann Sebastian Bach
(1685 - 1750)

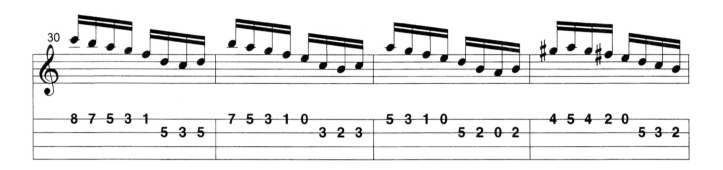

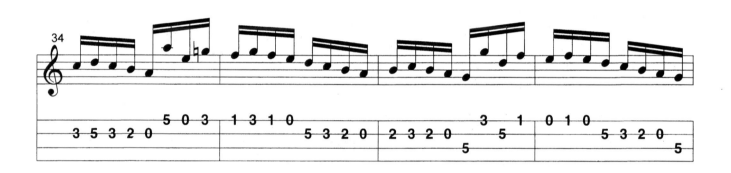

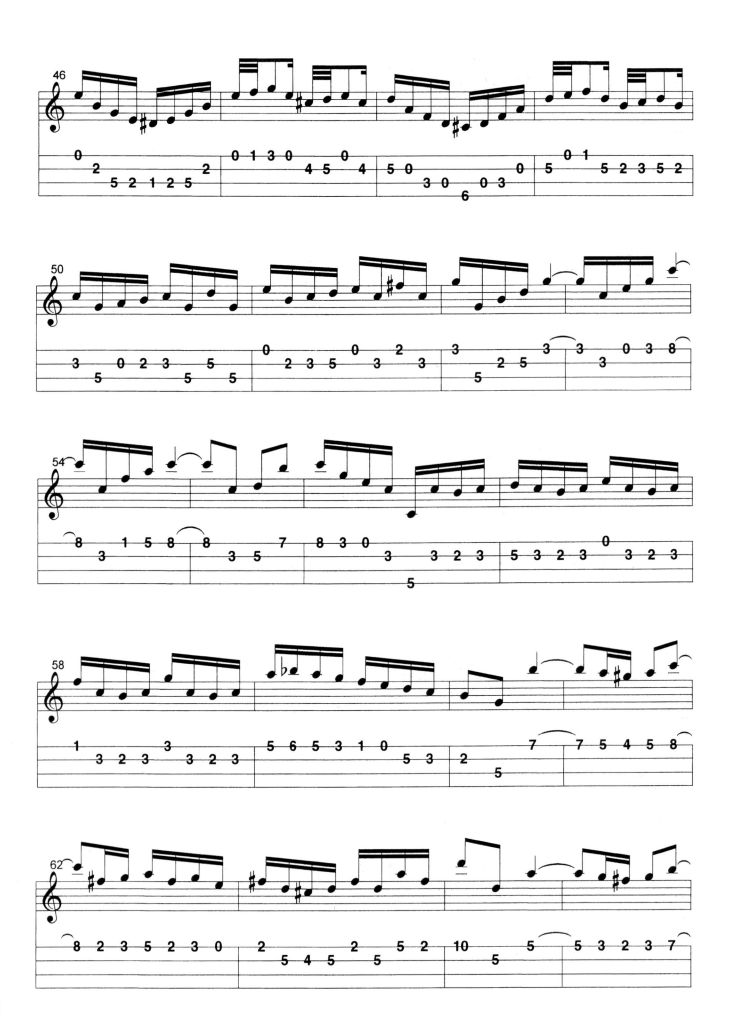

95

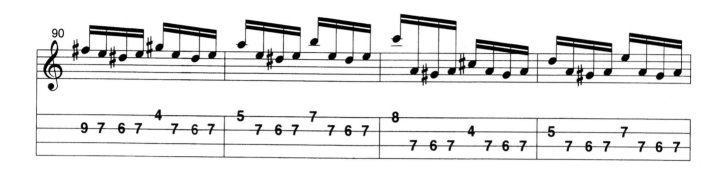

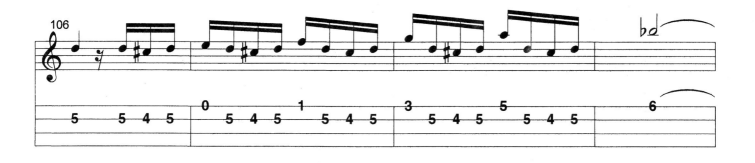
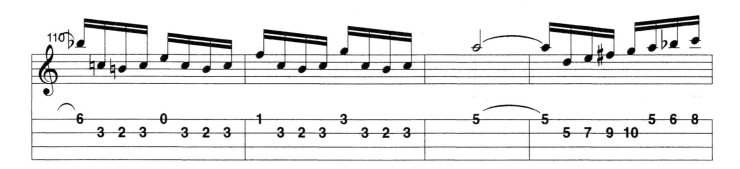
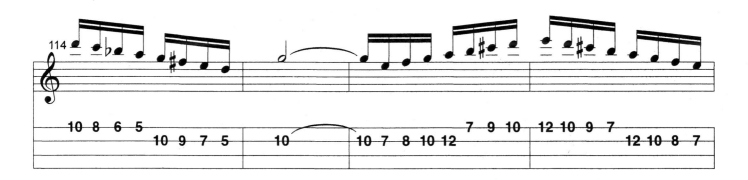
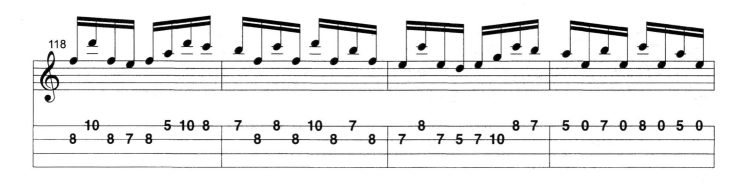

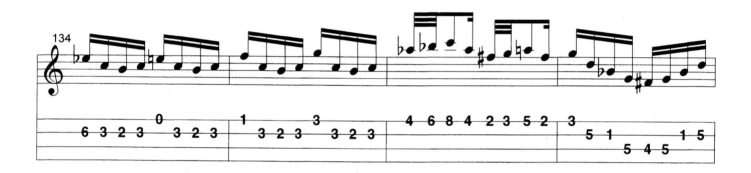

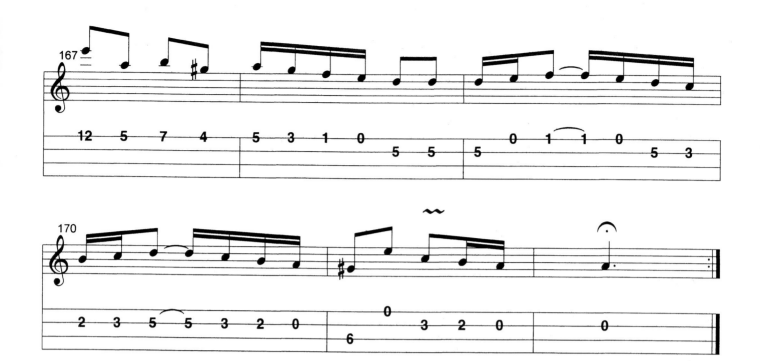

*This page has been
left blank to avoid
awkward page turns*

Sarabanda

(from Sonata No. 4 in D minor for solo Violin)

Johann Sebastian Bach
(1685 - 1750)